A TERRIBLE, HORRIBLE, NO GOOD YEAR

HUNDREDS OF STORIES ON THE PANDEMIC

BY TEACHERS, STUDENTS & PARENTS

EDITED BY LARRY SMITH

Six-Word Memoirs books may be ordered
through booksellers or by contacting:

Six-Word Memoirs
1663 Liberty Drive
Bloomington, IN 47403
www.sixwordmemoirs.com
866-577-887

Because of the dynamic nature of the Internet, any web
addresses or links contained in this book may have changed
since publication and may no longer be valid. The views
expressed in this work are solely those of the author and do
not necessarily reflect the views of the publisher, and the
publisher hereby disclaims any responsibility for them.

Any people depicted in stock imagery provided
by Getty Images are models, and such images are
being used for illustrative purposes only.
Certain stock imagery © Getty Images.

ISBN: 978-1-970183-00-9 (sc)
ISBN: 978-1-970183-02-3 (hc)
ISBN: 978-1-970183-01-6 (e)

Printed in the United States of America.

rev. date: 07/27/2021

"The brilliance is in the brevity."

- *The New York Post*

"Six-Word Memoirs have been lodged in the literary firmament."

- *Los Angeles Times*

"Will thrill minimalists and inspire maximalists."

- *Vanity Fair*

"A fabulously appealing exercise both for writers and for readers."

- *The Telegraph (London)*

"You can spend a lifetime brainstorming."

- *The New Yorker*

"Larry Smith is on a quest to spark the creativity of everyone."

- *Oprah Magazine*

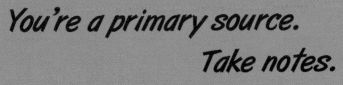

You're a primary source.

Take notes.

- Rebecca Klein, teacher

In the spring of 2008, shortly after the release of the first book of Six-Word Memoirs, *Not Quite What I Was Planning: Six-Word Memoirs by Writers Famous and Obscure*, I was invited to talk about storytelling with a group of third graders. And not just any third graders. These were the eight and nine year olds in my nephew Noah's class, a class located in the same elementary school where I learned long division.

That morning, the kids told stories, only now they did so six words at a time. They shared inner truths ("Nine years stacked within my soul"), self-reflections ("Born to be a spy, unknowable"), and wisdom beyond their years ("Life is better in soft pajamas"). A few days later, Noah ("Eight years old, combed hair twice") gave me a copy of the book his class had made: *Not Quite What We Were Planning: Six-Word Memoirs by Mrs. Nixon's Class*.

Why six? As I told the kids back in 2008 (and anyone else who asks me why all my T-shirts have six word stories on them), the idea of asking people to describe their lives in six words was inspired by a literary legend. As the story goes, Hemingway—a writer whose muscular style made each word count—was once challenged to write a whole novel in just six words. He came back with: "For sale: baby shoes, never worn." In a tweet on a new platform called Twittr (no "e" in Twitter back then), I gave the six-word challenge a personal twist and called these brief life stories Six-Word Memoirs. I saw how wonderful the constraint of six words could be as people responded to this challenge with brief stories that were poignant, memorable, and surprising. Fourteen years and more than one million six word stories later, Six-Word Memoirs has become a bestselling book series, a tool for self-expression in environments as varied as churches, therapy groups, weddings, and company meetings across the world. Above all, the six word form has become a way to spur on self-expression for anyone and everyone and has offered a simple way to discover the writer within.

In 2020, when COVID began to rage across the world, everything changed. For the first time in most of our lifetimes, we all experienced the same devastation and chaos. As the father of a fourth grader, I had a front-row seat to one particular piece of this new chaos: the total disruption of education.

As I saw my own son struggle with Zoom school and the heroic efforts of his teacher (whose perfect six are on page 59) I thought about how teachers, above all, seem to recognize the simple power of six words to unlock creativity, wrestle big ideas to the ground, and help kids make sense of their lives. With this in mind, I made a free teacher's guide on the Six-Word Memoir site, which was soon downloaded by thousands of teachers around the world and used to help kids process that unprecedented time.

A Terrible, Horrible, No Good Year includes many of the stories that were first shared in those classrooms. You'll also find contributions from teachers and parents about their experiences, along with a number of backstories we call "Lessons Learned"— stories that take us just a little bit deeper. And those illustrated Six-Word Memoirs popping off the pages? Many of these come from students at the Kansas City Art Institute, where Professor John Ferry has had a visual Six-Word Memoir assignment each semester since 2016. Other illustrations come from our younger artists and found their way to us through DrawTogether, a free, interactive art class for kids that the artist Wendy MacNaughton created at the start of the pandemic.

This tenth book in the Six-Word Memoir series also marks a new chapter in the six-word story. We've recently become part of Author Solutions, one of the world's largest self-publishing companies. Our plan? More or less the same as Mrs. Nixon's thirteen years ago: to provide the tools for any classroom, anywhere, to write and publish their own Six-Word Memoir books. Flip to the last page of this book for more on how this works.

And if you're wondering what happened to my nephew Noah, the kid who didn't comb his hair? He's now twenty-two, a recent college graduate, and the author of the memoir: "Next year: student becomes the teacher." As I write these words, Noah is about to embark on a career in education as a student teacher at Boston Arts Academy, a public high school with a focus on the arts.

We've all had a tough time during the pandemic. But Noah, and the many students, teachers, and parents who generously shared their stories in the pages that follow remind us that, to quote the very last memoir in this book, "Numbers rose, but sun did, too."

- Larry Smith, Berkeley, California, Fall 2021

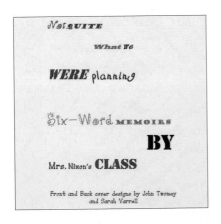

PANDEMIC: *zero out of five stars.*

- Penelope Williams, 11

Well,
    sure didn't see that coming.

- Alexis Davidson

This doesn't spark joy at all.

- Kimberly Ann Jardenil

FOMO is dead.
Hail to FOMI.

- Lorenzo Mattozzi

Mask on.
Zoom on.
PJs on.

- Sami Bell, 10

Thirteen lovies sleeping in my bed.

- Juno Bell, 6

Movie after movie.
Show after show.

- Asha Bell, 3

Taking staycation to the next level.

- Melissa Bell, Sami, Juno, and Asha's mom

I'm Googling New Zealand citizenship, *again.*

- W. Kamau Bell, Sami, Juno, and Asha's dad

I also social distance in dreams.

- Allyna Indab, former teacher

Teen social anxiety:
the new **black**.

- Delynn Parker

MY SANITY DIED
IN MY DOODLES.

- Miles D.

Cats attacking keyboards,
leaving gibberish behind.

- Elliott Cranmer, 11

3

Follow the stickers

Margin of error is six feet.

- Jessica Morgan

Please come closer;

too much space.

- Adele Spitz, 17

Six feet

never felt

so far.

- Ava Russ, 15

4

on **the** **ground.**

- *Delaney Jones, teacher*

Each death makes space for grief.

- *Chwen-Yuen Angie Chen*

Distance made me weak and **STRONG**.

- *Katrina Yrica C. Yso*

Desks apart, each one an igloo.

- *Beth David, teacher*

Stranded 9,000 miles away from home.

- *Sheryl Candol*

It goes over your nose, pal.

- *Stina Perkins*

He looked cuter with a mask.

- *Sara Abou Rashed*

You're not what I expected
maskless.

- *Nathan Florian*

Scared to take my
mask off.

- *Diya Patel, 12*

Not a criminal but running masked.

- Stella Kleinman, 17

Hey, is my mask
upside down?
nbside qomu¿

- Rob Brown

ROLLing eyes at those
couture masks.

- Elizabeth Mazer, 16

My EYES will do the SMILING.

- Roslyn Haley

- *Darshana Chandra, 10*

Finally, I can mute my teacher.

zoom® school
hrome BOOK
Padamas
desk
stress ball

- Lukas Smith, 10

COVID Couldn't Kill My Teaching Spirit

By Bobbie Jo Blackwell

Since childhood, school was the one place I always wanted to be. I was the youngest of nine and raised in a home wrought with addiction, abuse, and poverty. School was where I felt safe and valued, the one place where I allowed myself to believe in the impossible. My love of school—and especially reading—fueled me toward a career as a classroom teacher, and now, I strive to create the same love of school in my students.

Teaching in a Title I school allows me to work with kids from an array of backgrounds. Some are growing up in better circumstances than I did, while others have stories that make mine seem like a day in the park. Every year on the first day of school, I tell my own story to help students better relate to me and with the hope that my vulnerability will provide a sense of hope that might otherwise be missing. These are the first roots to take hold in our relationship and are key to both their successes and mine.

On the first day of the 2020-21 school year, I didn't tell my story. Something about doing so through a computer screen just felt disingenuous, and over those first six weeks, forming any type of connection seemed impossible. My time was consumed just getting kids to join class or begging them to participate once they did. I was in survivor mode, trying to fulfill the most basic of teaching obligations. The slapstick humor that I was accustomed to using was stifled. There were no crazy facial expressions intended to keep kids entertained and focused on me, and sneaking up on distracted students and whispering, "Whatcha doin?'" wasn't an option. Instead,

I trudged through, and at the end of each day, I cried buckets of tears, praying for the universe to shift in our favor. I needed my students back in the classroom with me as much as they needed to be there.

I'll never forget the excitement when, come October 2020, some students began attending in-person. Even though less than half of my students returned to the building, I was determined to make the most of it. I told the story of my childhood as if it was the first day of school. I told my students how reading had saved my life. And I watched something light up in them. Finally, the seeds of hope and connection were planted.

Having students in the building breathed life into me. We formed bonds that will forever be woven into the fabric of who we are. We had an extraordinary year, one that I knew had to end in a very special way. I am the teacher who teaches to the very last day, and I have always attempted to find a meaningful way to end the year, one that allows students a final opportunity to stretch their thinking and utilize their skills while having fun. This year I knew it had to be something incredible, and after much searching, I stumbled on Six-Word Memoirs.

As I watched my students find joy in constructing six-word glimpses into the most pivotal year of their lives, the pain of the experience lifted, replaced by a sense of healing. I saw into the hearts of some of my students for the very first time. I laughed with some, cried for others, and was left speechless by many of my students' reflections on their years. As the distance between us closed, a part of me was healed, and, I like to think, a part of my students was healed as well. COVID couldn't kill my teaching spirit just like it couldn't kill my students' capacity to learn, grow, and teach me about the power of vulnerability and connection.

Bobbie Jo Blackwell is a sixth-grade reading/writing teacher at Burbank Middle School, a Title I school, in Houston, Texas.

This was one big emotional rollercoaster. - *Mercedes Torres*

Headline News: COVID hacked 6th grade. - *Gilbert Flores*

Honestly, I have seen better years. - *Genesis Cervantes*

Connectivity issues disconnected
teachers from me. - *Phoenix Galicia*

Depression is more depressing
without hugs. - *Maya Sanchez*

Mental stability or perfect grades?
Choose. - *Kalubi Castillo*

Faking my way through the pandemic. - *Damian Conejo*

Give me a break. I'm tired. - *Paulina Bautista*

This year was kind of sad. - *Xavier Ramirez*

Great experience—
 but no repetition please. - *Kymberly Galvan*

Went back to school. It's cool! - *Luis Sanchez*

I let COVID steal my personality. - *Allareli Alvarez*

Last minute...just like my projects. - *Michelle Alonso*

Sometimes we have to admit defeat. - *Eddie Torres*

COVID couldn't kill my teaching spirit. - *Ms. Blackwell*

Masked sixth graders in the homerooms of Bobbie Jo Blackwell, Clara Bujnoch, and Eric McDaniel at Burbank Middle School, Houston, Texas.

Cats cuddle.
Students struggle.
Online school.

- Audrey Zimmermann, 9

I missed FRIENDS,
but not school.

- Harrison Zimmermann, 7

**Isolation makes me
appreciate my home.**

*- Kate Zimmermannn, Audrey and
Harrison's mom*

Forced family time:
COVID's disguised blessing.

- Kevin Zimmermann, Audrey and Harrison's dad

The world

has never felt

smaller.

- Maggie Smith

*Studying and parenting
is never easy.*

- Charramae Cruz

Parents to students
all over again.

- Jackielyn Eronico

The greatest gift:
motherhood amidst pandemic.

- Cheryl Martelino

Why are my kids so LOUD?

- Lesley Swick

Teacher finding inspiration through uneasy times.

- April Goodman, teacher

When everything
goes *wrong,*
do *right.*

- Jannen M. Cabañog, 19

Emancipating the room from
pandemic challenges.

- Lheojr Dogomeo, teacher

Getting handle on pandemic.
Need lid.

- Krystyna Fedosejevs

THERE'S
TIME
TO
FISH
IN
ISOLATION

- Colete Martin, Kansas City Art Institute, Teaching Assistant

CREATION
in
solitude

Led
Me
Here

Internet down:
the new "snow day."

- Jennifer Lopez, teacher

MY BAD CONNECTION ATE MY HOMEWORK.

- Christy Page, teacher

**When connection fails,
breathe and return.**

- Mikaela Jane Dagani

Synchronous. Asynchronous. Hybrid.
Virtual. Zoom hell.

- Shelley Moran, teacher

I FEEL WARMTH THROUGH THE PIXELS.

- Phoenix Thomas, 16

Make-up tutorial vlogging makes
me sane.

- Janah Marie Osorio

**Discovered my
hidden talent for
rebooting.**

- Meg Sencil

We made Zoom our fairy tale.

- Rehani Slipock, teacher

Technology Made Things Harder, Then Easier

By *Michelle Wolff*

I am an English teacher in a suburban high school in Michigan. When it was starting to look like we might be forced to close down last year, many of us—like so many teachers across the world—were unprepared for the task. I for one wasn't ready to seamlessly switch to online teaching any more than the majority of my students were ready to switch to online learning. Ready or not, on March 13, 2020 we had our last day in school for four months.

I had always planned to have a better online presence for students. Yet as a busy teacher trying to get through each day, week, month … it just didn't happen. Until it did overnight. I joined a lot of the world in learning about Zoom meetings. I discovered Schoology, Google Classroom, CommonLit, Khan Academy, Edmentum, and Remind. I had a crash course in all of them and, much to my chagrin, realized my tolerance level with new technology was pretty low. It was even lower for many of my students. Through numerous tears and the limitless support and help from my colleagues, I got the hang of it and then helped my students do the same. Establishing a new routine was good for all of us.

And then something unexpected happened: I found that I was able to connect with kids in a new, quite special way. The quiet kids in person were often more eager to speak and interact online. The students who like time to think about their responses flourished with discussion boards and individual emails. I was able to give my students more one-on-one attention. My visual learners roared with laughter at my first attempts at teaching with the help of YouTube videos. Above all, the lessening of requirements allowed me to interact more meaningfully with my students since we had less pressure to focus on all the standardized tests. Getting to know my students, and letting them into my "home," was a challenge, for sure. And ultimately a joy.

I've been able to use the technology I adapted last year to benefit the students this year as well. I managed to keep my students connected while growing as a teacher and taking my new skill set into the future of my career. What will my classroom look like in the next decade? I have no idea. But I do know that together we will be ready for anything.

Michelle Wolff teaches English at L'Anse Creuse High School in Harrison Township, Michigan. A regular contributor to sixwordmemoirs.com, she has written more than 2,800 six-word stories—and counting.

 Six-Word Memoirs **from Mrs. Wolff's students**

Isolation; Not the same as space. - *Emily B.*

Isolation is not a new feeling. - *Enrico W.*

Surrounded by people, but completely alone. - *Rachel K.*

Mental Health completely ruined by COVID. - *Victoria L.*

Screen time is over thirteen hours. - *Hannah B.*

Three scares, four families, zero deaths. - *John G.*

We all took 2019 for granted. - *Lexus P.*

Life changed when it stopped moving. - *Mackenzie B.*

Every touch, felt like a risk. - *Danny E.*

Distance gives reasons to love harder. - *Emily F.*

Are you there?

Are you there?

- Lynn Adam Ripley, teacher

You're muted.

You're MUTED.

YOU'RE MUTED.

- Annie Rowell

Sorry miss, *my video isn't working.*

- Christopher Liu, 15

I'm sorry,
I was on mute.

- Kay Raye

Mustering a performance for
muted avatars.

- Humaira Zakaria, teacher

Technology is helpful.
Humans are essential.

- Kevin Mullins, teacher

You're in My caMeRa! GET OUT!!!

- Cassie Evans

Online school was
loading, loading,
loading...

- Bree Hervas, 7

We just ran out of data!

- Vickie Breeden

Zoom school? I'd rather eat rocks.

- Bean Abrams

Voices explode from screens, seeking escape.

- *Viv Mansbach, 13*

Slowly turning into a technological potato.

- *Jad Ammar*

Students right now: virtual space prisoners.

- *Aliza Beloria, 20*

Zoom's notification sounds haunt my dreams.

- *Rachel Hardin, teacher*

ENDLESS COMPUTER SCREENS, ENDLESSLY MAKING ART.

Extra time...
TAUGHT MYSELF
3D MODELING!

Jessi Macko,
Kansas City Art Institute

Proof of life: turn on camera.

- Alessaundrei Christer Villamala, 18

Eyes aching because of
online learning

- Izabella Christer Villamala, 12

Life is still here; cherish it!

- Mhalou Villamala,
Alessaundrei and
Izabella's mom

Noun: Zoom

Verb: Zoom

Adjective: Zoom

- Jennifer Schneider, teacher

Rona ruins school, so does Monday.

- Jack C., 15

Same movie watched over
ten times.

- Keyvanna B., 14

Are you okay?
Now, onto Shakespeare.

- Rachel Lloyd, Jack and Keyvanna's teacher

I have mastered the pandemic mullet.

- Erin C. Scussel, teacher

Now I'm a barber. Who knew?

- John Tehan

Life's too short,
dye your hair.

- Julia Dinah Solajes

EveRyday is a **bad haiR** day.

- Leigh Giza

Discovered patience the size of
EVEREST.
- Carla Cabahug

A gripping, outlandish way to survive.
- John Harrell, 13

There are BIG responsibilities being nine.
- Jude Dominique, 9

Protected kids mental health,
NEGLECTED MINE.
- Kelly Croasmun

My son's pandemic resilience revived me.

- Larry Smith

Pandemic bonds inter-generational book club buddies.

- Carol Smith, Larry's mom

Zoom Academy: teaching granddaughter or me?

- Kim Mitchell

Your siblings are your best cheatmates.

- Jada Mancera, 12

Hugged my grandson through a window.

- Ken Stasiak

Sadly, kids seem quieter after COVID.

- Mario Montanaro, teacher

Holding it together only in public.

- Amie Livengood, teacher

There is no place like home.

- Krizzia Regulacion

We're home; let's have a conversation.

- Jo Ann Daniels

Our children are not nice people.

- Caroline Ann Gonzalez

I *love* and *hate* my family.

- Sadie McMahon, 10

Couldn't punish "go to your room."

- Joel Stein

- Carene Casey Tiaga, 11

- D'Andre Paul Tiaga, 8

- Ada Fleischmann, 10

We Will (Eventually) Rock You Again

By Chelsea Moosekian

I'm a drummer and a music educator in New Orleans. And yeah, I'm a grownup, but the unimportance of that is a big reason why I teach music to kids. In music class, kids don't need me to tell them anything. When you put on "We Will Rock You" or "Cissy Strut," nobody—five or fifty—needs "instruction." They tune in. They rock out. I'm an afterthought. The music speaks for itself.

In my classes, I like to bring in one special instrument—a snare drum, say—to pass around. Each kid handles it while we talk about the instrument as a group. They get to hold it, touch it, and most importantly play this thing that they're usually told to leave alone. They get to see their peers do things they'd never think of, *and* they get to practice listening to each other. Because music is just as much about space to listen, space to observe, as it is about making noise.

I remember the first time I brought a bass drum into a kindergarten class, how the kids crowded around, sticking their heads *inside* the drum while somebody played. I remember the virtuoso first grader who, when the electric guitar got to him, absolutely shredded the lick from "Seven Nation Army." I remember countless show-and-tells at the Green Preschool, where more than half the class brought in harmonicas.

When the pandemic hit, all of it stopped. Those first virtual months when our students were at home were actually okay, school-wise. Even though Zoom doesn't do squat for collective sound activities (you try singing along with twenty kids on a screen), I made videos of myself playing songs my students knew. I sent instructions on how to play the songs, which kids (and parents) loved; it was an activity they could do together as a family. Instruments at home? Get 'em out! No instruments? Bring on the pots and pans!

It was when we got back to the classroom that I had the toughest time. We weren't allowed to sing. Singing in the time of Covid is a high-risk activity. I showed up with my snare drum and a canister of Lysol wipes, but the school told me no, even with precautions, we weren't allowed to pass instruments. I had rooms full of kids looking at me like, *What are we supposed to do now? Listen to you?* And, I was with them. I didn't want them to listen to me. I didn't want to listen to me. I wanted *us* to listen to *music*.

So, I turned to those old days of rocking out to Queen and tried some history-based classes. We made playlists. We watched videos. We started with Jimi Hendrix, and while we couldn't pass around the electric guitar while we did it, we could listen to his songs and learn about his life. We studied Trombone Shorty, a New Orleans legend, and Carla Azar, a badass drummer I love. I let kids ask to study musicians they were interested in, and together, we listened.

As I write this, it's early June 2021 and we're allowed to sing outside, but we're still not allowed to pass instruments. I'm not going to lie, I haven't found a good alternative, and I can't wait for the restrictions to be lifted so we can sit around and listen to the first lines of "All Along the Watchtower," and I can crack open that black vinyl case and hand that shiny red guitar over to a three-year-old. Because that moment? That moment is why I teach. I don't think they'd care if Jimi himself was in the room talking at them. In that moment, they can't hear about music from somebody else. They know it for themselves.

Chelsea Moosekian is a drummer and music educator. She plays with The Daiquiri Queens, Nick Shoulders, Cinder Well, and many more bands. She lives and works in New Orleans

K-Pop: saving lives note by note.

- Zoe Hart, 16

TikToking my way out
of this.

- Ron Dilbert

**Be the remote of
your life.**

- Abbygail Ariola

I used to like the silence.

- Livia Charles Basche, 12

QUOTA OF FAMILY
TIME WAS EXCEEDED.

- *Dana Calvo*

Early argument in morning
hits differently.

- Louriel Johmary Quiachon, 16

Getting opinionated.
Realized they're
all grownups.

- Jana Philips, Louriel's mom

My teacher teaches better than mom.

- Xander Anunciado, 5

How do teachers
manage little monsters?

- Suzette Anerson, Xander's mom

I was not trained for this.

- Kyle Martin, teacher

Proof I can't be a teacher!

- Lucy Flowers

I became a teacher,
babysitter, storyteller.

- Alberto Loyola

Pandemic epiphany:
teachers are sorely underpaid.

- Mishell DeFelice

As the principal at Montalvo Elementary School in Ventura, California, I've had a very professional and personal lens into the world of bilingual education. And what most people don't realize about bilingual education is that it's not just about the language. Yes, there's something wonderful about watching kids who were once monolingual evolve into kids who speak, play, and think in two languages. But the magic of dual immersion education is in the exchange, the act of giving one thing and receiving something equally valuable in return. At a school like mine, where students are 30 percent native Spanish speakers, 30 percent native English speakers, and 30 percent bilingual, the exchange is not only linguistic but cultural.

Walk into a classroom and you'll see five year olds on the rug, cabezas juntas, sharing items from home that match the letter of the week. Go out on the playground and you'll see Asha (African American), Mireya (Persian), and Maria (from El Salvador) having to work hard at verbal communication but effortlessly playing an intricate game of tag they created together. At Christmas, you might find an English speaker invited to a Spanish speaker's house to make tamales, and when we celebrate Dia del Nino, all the families come together to share food and tell stories.

That all stopped when COVID hit. Suddenly kids were on Zoom, which is no way for any kid to learn, but it's especially problematic when you're trying to learn a language. To acquire language, babies mirror their parents. They try things out. They play. There is an organic interchange. But when kids got stuck behind a screen, they became passive recipients of information instead of active participants in a dynamic exchange. These kids lost over a year of authentic language acquisition, but they lost something else equally, if not more, important: they stopped valuing one of these two languages. In a world where English is the default, kids no longer had a place where Spanish was just as valuable as English.

We value *lo que se habla*. We value what is spoken—what is literally being communicated but also what is represented by this communication, two rich cultures that in this divided world often stay unknown to each other. When COVID struck, the cultural divide became even greater. As we return to the classrooms, bilingual and monolingual alike, we need to find ways back to each other so that we can once again know the endless value of these students who we teach, learn from, and watch learn from each other.

Claudia Caudill is the principal of Montalvo Elementary School in Ventura, California, and is Lauren and Truman's mom.

Try being quarantined...
with the PRINCIPAL!

- *Lauren and Truman Caudill, 10*

VIRTUAL TEACHING: FRUSTRATING PROCESS, LIONHEARTED STUDENTS.

- John Ferry, Kansas City Art Institute, Professor

Teaching is hard.
Remote teaching harder.

- Ellis Reyes, teacher

Grace is more important than grades.

- Lisa Casillas, teacher

**Online, saw myself
from students'
viewpoint.**

- Camille Smith, teacher

Pandemic Teaching Curriculum:
resilience, courage, love.

- Kate Zimmermann, teacher

Trapped smiles play hide and seek.

- Van G. Garrett, teacher

Reminiscing: the smell
of chalk dust.

- Rachel Paula Celis

Teachers: experiencing
home life with them.

- Nicole Busch, teacher

It's **ALL ABOUT** showing you care.

- Samantha Tanner, teacher

Mask Pivot: Smile With Your Eyes

Everyone made due,
teachers and students alike,
displayed humanity,
kindness, and support
for one another despite
the stifling of mask wearing,
unable to share and show
their smiles to each other,
somehow pivoting
and learning to connect
through wide-eye smiles
of squints and eyebrow lifts.

- Meghan Adler
Literacy Specialist, Hudson Valley, NY

Great moms aren't always
great teachers.

- Teo Rojas Cann, 11

Impossible to fret on a trampoline.

- *Piper Kerman*

Extrovert became introvert.
Hesitant to revert.

- *Ann Miller-Tobin*

Read every book in
the house.

- *Francesca Gomez-Novy, 12*

Realized I was happier staying home.

- *Austin Crisman*

Dessert for breakfast. Wine for lunch.

- Chris Farber

PJs, Zoom, and snacks. That's life.

- Julia Duzynski

Home Ec: rationing
butter, bourbon, sanity.

- Christine Triano

Social distancing myself from
the fridge.

- Maria Leopoldo

Required school supplies:
screens,
screens,
screens.

- Emil Dashiel, teacher

Daytime pajamas make great
school attire.

- Audrey Heath, 11

Student is typing...
time is passing.

- Christopher Fouche, teacher

"Gotta go to the bathroom brb."

- Sydne Arnold, teacher

What

a

lovely

community

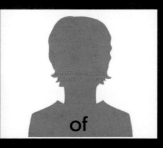
of

rectangles!

- Sean Keller, teacher

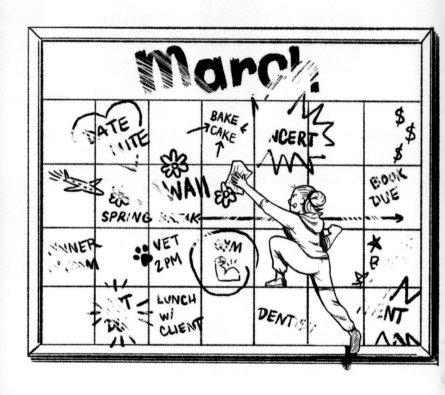

Time isn't real, so who cares.

- *MacKenzie Fulmer, Kansas City Art Institute*

JOKES?

AT A TIME LIKE THIS?

- Aspen Mayor, Kansas City Art Institute

AWESOME! No shower required for classes!

- Channing Dale, 21

Good thing Zoom
doesn't include
aromascope.

*- Laureatte Loy,
Channing's mom*

**Miss you mama,
please come home.**

- Chase Farrell, 3

My son named his cellphone "Mama."

- Vanessa Marzo, Chase's mom

Masks Protect Us From Farts, Too.

By Ruby Bryan

I teach in a small therapeutic day program for students who have severe emotional and behavioral impairments, and my classroom has the youngest kids—kindergarten through third grade. To give you an idea of the severity of their needs, the staff to student ratio in our classrooms is 1:2. Programs like this are in a very small niche on the special education continuum, so I'm no stranger to extreme behaviors. But there's one behavior that in twenty-seven years of teaching, I've yet to find a way to mitigate: the disruptive power of a student's fart.

I can put systems in place that reward students for ignoring many different types of behaviors, and believe me, the students I work with have quite a range of displays, but student farts are something that remain constant, year in and year out.

They love to fart and they love to do it as close to students and teachers as possible. Loud, deliberately noisy farts, accompanied by immense gloating and a terrific sense of pride are a regular part of my day. But with masks now required at school, it's me who's pointing my finger and laughing: Ha ha, joke's on you! Because guess what kids? Masks protect from farts, too.

Ruby Bryan is a teacher in a public school district in the Midwest.

You're in school, out of bed!

- *Cassandra May, teacher*

"Can't, I'm sick"
works too well.

- *Arrow Hill, 19*

Your Google doc didn't
spontaneously erase.

- *Michelle Rennix, teacher*

It's fourth period already, WAKE UP!

- *D.S. Kramer*

Professor contemplates.
Who's behind the screens?

- *Stephen Rosenbaum*

Remote teaching not even
remotely successful.

- *Darcy Grabenstein*

Mute,
    mute,
  mute;
remove from meeting.

- *Ash-Lee Covey, teacher*

Homework due at 11:59.
Submitted 12:03.

- *Kaitlin Gannon*

Tiger King, Schitt's Creek, Ted Lasso.

- Krish Mukerjee

<u>Syllabus:</u>
coffee, zoom,
MSNBC, Netflix,
wine.

- Elisa Shevitz

Enrolled at culinary school
called YouTube.

- Cynthia Murillo

I've been everywhere thanks to television.

- Tuesday Nichols, teacher

Cleaned Lysol container with Lysol wipe.

- Angela Weisser Moore

Traded homegrown avocados
for toilet paper.

- JL Nuss

Stocked up on TP and humanity.

- Heather Nakasuji

Have binged all
seasons. Now what?

- Cleo Quart Maass, 9

Next year:
    student becomes the teacher.

- Noah Michaud, student teacher

Volunteer pod mom: refilled
emptying nest.

- Saralee Michaud, Noah's mom

My heart misses a MILLION people.

- Lucette Cortese, 5

Lockdown's got nothing on single moms.

- Chiara Cortese, Lucette's mom

I am a mental health counselor based at a public elementary school in the San Francisco Bay Area. During the pandemic, boundaries around my work disintegrated as I got to know families in new ways while together we grappled to support children through unprecedented challenges. A lot of what I saw, you would expect—Fortnite addiction, missing meals typically provided at school, anxiety about COVID-19—and there were resources to address those things. But then there were consequences specific to this pandemic, ones I hadn't trained for or even considered before.

During the first six months of the shelter-in-place, many children displayed a resistance to joy that perplexed their families. Parents got incredibly creative at planning ways for kids to get outside, see their friends safely, and have fun. They organized bike rides, cupcakes, and kickball matches, but what followed was depressed sulking and epic tantrums.

Why were kids seemingly triggered by their favorite things? I believe it was grief.

In the beginning stages of grief, we are still processing our loss. We need to mourn and memorialize before we can move on. The ongoing uncertainty of what was coming next during the pandemic coupled with the filters we adults tend to apply to our communications with kids about scary things made mourning and memorializing nearly impossible for children. Hearing parents laugh and even feeling their own spirits lift temporarily was threatening to children, perhaps because they feared that everyone around them would accept this new normal and they would be left alone in this new devastating place, wishing for how things used to be. Refusing to see friends and resisting innovative improvements to the sheltering lifestyle was a way of reminding adults: *this is not okay!*

And then there was Zoom school. Elementary school is a stimulating environment that consistently engages all five senses throughout a child's day, and children benefit from sharing that experience with their peers. I cannot stress enough how many daily, vital opportunities for growth and learning were lost by reducing school to a two-dimensional digital experience. Hearing their favorite song played on the playground and feeling brave enough to be the first to start dancing, trying a new breakfast muffin and looking to the other kids to gauge their own reaction to the taste—these experiences help children develop their sense of self. Many children recognized distance learning for the joke it was and discovered that no teachers could stop them from simply snapping their Chromebooks shut when they had had enough.

Now imagine being a *kindergartener* in March of 2020. That year at home made up such a significant portion of their lives that in person school was like a distant dream by the end. We did our best to remind them it was real, and I'm so grateful for the staff at the school where I work because they understood that the best thing we could do with that digital window was to help kids maintain an emotional connection to their community.

I remember there was one day when, because of nearby wildfires in the Bay Area, it stayed dark all day and the sky was a deep, smoky orange. It was one of those times where you think, "I may never experience anything this surreal for the rest of my life." I wanted so badly for the kids to feel what it was like to be at school, so I spent the whole day running up and down the empty hallways, brandishing my laptop at the windows and yelling at kids on Zoom: "Look at that! Can you believe it? The playground looks like it's inside a jack-o-lantern!" If we couldn't all be there in person—grieving, playing, mourning, and finding moments of joy—I wanted the kids to remember that this was still a shared experience and despite the digital distance, we were all going through this together.

Ivy Smyth is a mental health counselor at an elementary school in San Francisco Bay Area public school system.

I BUBBLED EVERY

NG UP INSIDE ME

- Samantha Brennan, Kansas City Art Institute

Teaching kindergarten online: still a circus.

- Julie Driscoll Waskiewicz,
teacher

Can't share toys over
Google Meet.

- Jennifer Henderson, teacher

Teacher and tech support in one.

- Ashley Gallaugher, teacher

Pandemic teaching is like herding cats.

- Christina Lahr, teacher

Are you there?
Hello,
hello,
hello?

- Michael C. Blevit, teacher

Bueller....?
You're too young
for that.

- Victoria Kraft Shafer, teacher

Hun, you are still on mute.

- Alison Golian, teacher

I'm sitting here talking to myself.

- Emily Hyatt Olds, teacher

F*ck, F*ck, F*ck, F*ck, F*ck, F*ck.

- Ozzie S., 11

My heart sings; I have a writer.

- Dylan S., Ozzie's dad

**Eighth hour of YouTube.
Send Help!**

- Leela Chandra, 12

Wait, don't we have
screen limits?

- Melanie Abrams, Leela's mom

I regret saying, *"I hate school."*

- Riana Heffron, 14

Children
needed me.
I cried often.

- Debbie Stainbrook

TEACHING:
leave it to the professionals.

- Jenny Lagumbay

Missing the
afternoon school
bells ringing.

- Analyn M. Piañar

Library Locked. May I Borrow You?

By Jess deCourcy Hinds

As a school librarian I think the moment that the pandemic hit me hardest was when my dean said, "The library will be locked all year. No one will be able to borrow books." What would happen to all the unloved books and stories?

I adore digital research, but when I founded the library at Bard High School Early College Queens twelve years ago, I built my community around books. We're located in the most diverse borough of New York City and, indeed, the most diverse place in the world. Thirty-four languages are spoken on campus. When I returned in September 2020 (I was "returning" as a virtual librarian after a maternity leave), I was desperate to once again get books into students' hands and bring us together again.

Most colleagues were working remotely like me, but a handful showed up in person. There were only about sixty of six hundred students in the building, unlike other schools across the country with higher return rates. I couldn't imagine how desolate the usually packed halls would feel, how lonely those sixty students would feel walking past a dark, shuttered library. For the first few days, I shipped books to students' homes and even delivered some in my baby's stroller. But I wasn't reaching enough people. So, I bolstered my Guest Writers series, inviting authors to speak on one of the students' favorite topics: immigrant and LGBTQIA+ narratives.

One of our first poets was Jiwon Choi, a preschool teacher in Brooklyn and author of two collections of poetry. In her poem, "One Daughter Is Worth Ten Sons," Choi writes about the Korean tradition of girls washing "ghosts" out of the family's rice. This is both an honor and burden, and it resonated with students who also felt confined by cultural and gender roles.

In "Korean Grocery," the narrator deals with unrequited love in the frozen fish aisle where she "press[ed] frozen halibut to my hot flesh."

"Why'd you do *that*, Jiwon?" one student demanded. Everyone cracked up.

I tried to maintain decorum. "Do you mean, 'Why did Jiwon's *narrator* put fish on her skin?"

Jiwon laughed. "No, that's okay," she said. "I confess—the weirdo in the poem is me." Even over Zoom, I could feel the students' delight and their relief that someone else was odder than they were.

Luke Dani Blue (they/them) is the author of the forthcoming short story collection, *Pretend It's My Body* and Zoomed in from Alberta, Canada. After we read a story in which a trans person crosses the country in a Greyhound bus, my student, J., read his meticulously crafted question from the chat: "You and your characters seem to thrive and dream of uncertain circumstances because they hold so much possibility, yet very often in life we are disappointed and miscalculate the trajectory of our new paths. What would you say is your margin of error when it comes to dream versus actual trajectory?" Blue was so stunned by the question, all they could say was, "Woah, I feel so *seen* by that question. I'm going to have to think about that one."

There were many moments when authors felt exposed, when a question brought up something almost too personal, but they usually pushed on and answered anyway. And I've become more open, too. I've learned to lend *myself* as a librarian. As I've worked with more students suffering from depression, I've admitted that I too have suffered from the curse. As students confide in me about their sexual and gender identities, I've come out as queer for the first time in my career. My students and I have a new sense of ease with each other. We cry together now, but we laugh a lot more too.

One of my students, R., I've known by two different sets of pronouns and three names. Every day I'm proud to see R. getting closer and closer to their authentic self. Days before their graduation, I was hit by a wave of nostalgia. "Remember ninth grade?" I said. "Remember how you kneeled down by your favorite shelf, and *hugged* the bookcase?" "I do!" my student laughed. This memory gave me an ache for the time we lost when the library was closed.

You can't ever lock up a library. A library can be an exchange of odd vulnerabilities and truths, a question and answer. As long as people can still come together to share stories and words, libraries can be everywhere.

Jess deCourcy Hinds, the Library Director of Bard High School Early College Queens, is completing a novel about queer graffiti artists in post-9/11 New York.

YouTube:

negligent coparent,

inattentive teacher,

savior.

- Elan Lee

MY NEIGHBORS

- Camille Fellers, Kansas City Art Institute

DADDY, go put on some PANTS!

- Hazel Hoffman, 11

Big plans today:
oh, never mind.

- Audrey Hoffman, 13

Made the bread,
sometimes the bed.

- Julie Oppenheimer,
Hazel and Audrey's mom

Where the F are the taquitos?

- Joseph Daiber, 15

Yes sweetie, Cheez-Its
count as protein.

- Sonia Marcus

Major COVID-19 symptom:
sourdough bread making.

- Leetha Filderman

Online school: eating vegetables without
dessert.

- Daria Shepelavy, 15

I wish I had a cat.

- Lula Silva, 5

I wish I had a dog.

- Leo Silva, 8

Mom, can we get a puppy?

- Lily Lefkow, 19

You sure you want one, Mom?

- Coco Lefkow, 17

Why did we get a puppy?

- Laurel Lefkow, Lily and Coco's mom

Humans Are My Number One Fear

By Nava Krieger

Wow. I cannot believe that it was nine years ago that I was brought into the Six-Word Memoir world. In fourth grade, my art teacher gave my class an assignment to work on a Six-Word Memoir. Mine was: "Bears Are My Number One Fear." A lot has happened in the past nine years of my life. I graduated from both middle and high school. I became an aunt. I traveled to many new countries. And I saw the world completely change before my eyes.

In 2012, I thought the biggest problem I would face was bears. Even though I was scared of them, I knew they too have feelings and were probably just as scared as I was. I am eighteen now and know that there are bigger things to be afraid of, and nothing has been more terrifying than COVID.

The pandemic has changed everyone's lives: children, teens, adults, and even dogs. Since I had to stay at home all the time, I started to notice things I would not have normally seen. One of these things was that after a while my puppy, Oreo, did not want yet another walk with me and seemed to miss her weekly hike with her doggy friends. I noticed that she was having a hard time being with the same people all the time. And I noticed all of this because I was in the same situation.

Nava Krieger is a senior at YULA Girls High School in Los Angeles.

I never thought I could actually fear being around people; the most natural thing in the world for me is to be social. Then the coronavirus put everything on hold, pushing us back into our own isolated worlds. At nine, I feared bears. At eighteen something even scarier happened: I feared humans.

2012

2021

"Hey, stop licking the camera please."

- Christi Berghofer, teacher

"Please stop spinning in
your chair."

- Alison Golian, teacher

Please stop changing
your screen name.

- Derek Rhody, teacher

"Please clothe student,
self, and family."

- Charis Kipepo, teacher

"Dog toys don't go in mouths."

- *Amanda Borowski, teacher*

"Can you see my screen now?"

- *Amy Nealon, teacher*

"That's not what chat is for!"

- *Jenny Cantrell, teacher*

"Get your cat off your keyboard."

- *Sam Kassel, teacher*

Cut my own bangs.

Bad decision.

- *Mabel Hartman, 14*

- Alessaundrei Christer Villamala, 18

Zoom kindergarten
    broke us,
    built us.

- *Rachel Sklar*

I taught math; they
    taught resiliency.

- *Loryn Gavula, teacher*

My teacher is funnier in
three-dimensions.

- *James Lyons, 10*

Resilience built one Zoom after another.

- *Cathy Bamji*

Skipped the homework. No one noticed.

- Kira Ivy Mazer, 11

Hiding in basement.
Don't tell children.

- Laura Mazer, Kira's mom

Me not so ~~smart~~ due to
pandemic.

- Laszlo Stein, 12

Took my son's exams way seriously.

- Carla Cabahug

Son barely did anything.
Graduated anyway.

> - *Neal Pollack*

**Virtual semester.
Their best grades ever.**

> - *David Brown*

Did not shop for school supplies.

> - *Sheryl Candol*

Still haven't seen my own campus.

> - *Mary Elizabeth Williams*

For Sale:

prom dress,

never worn.

- Caroline Richardson, 19

Learned to script, made many zombies.

- *Teo Siegel-Acevedo, 11*

HELP! Roblox zombies ate my kid!

- *Deborah Siegel-Acevedo, Teo's mom*

Who's that Lady heRe? Oh, MoM...

- *Zechariah Fetterman, 7*

Found out I have
two kids.

- *Lisa Q. Fetterman,*
  Zechariah's mom

One cough could change your life.

- Ashley Ells, 17

Testing: **positive**...wait,
negative...stupid test.

- Karla Frischke, 11

Celebrated birthday; only me
at home.

- Glenvic O. Bacala

Birthday cake. No candles. Thanks, COVID.

- Anna McCutcheon

COVID therapy garden now feeding neighbors.

- *Ellen Card, teacher*

Finally meeting neighbors after eight years.

- *Jaylene Henderson*

Grateful for outdoor playgroups.

Onward, upward!

- *Jesse Carmichael*

Never take seeing friends for granted.

- *Sylvia Carbone, 10*

Was catlike:
napped,
ate,
avoided humans.

- Liam Chapman, 10

His voice unmuffled

The beautiful sound

- Zoe Richardson, Kansas City Art Institute

lost
some friends

and found myself.

**Senior class president.
No senior classes.**

- Whisper Schroeder, 18

It's really lonely performing for
nobody.

- Aleksandr Schroder, 23

Two shots: not just for
parties!

*- Sheila Schroder,
Whisper and Aleksandr's mom*

Kids' worlds upended; a father worries.

- Eric Schroeder, Whisper and Aleksandr's dad

Reinvented Teaching When My Toolbox Disappeared

By Danielle Kardon

My classes are small (four students at a time, sometimes two depending on group dynamics), the classroom I teach in is the size of a kid's bedroom, and my students aren't allowed to take work home with them, because there is no "home with them." My students range from fourteen to eighteen years old and are incarcerated. When we're in class together, it's in the detention facility where they also eat, sleep, study, and do just about everything else that comprises the life of a teenager.

Despite their situation, my students aren't so different from students in traditional schools. They want to learn, they want to engage, they want to be seen as whole people. They struggle with self-esteem and work hard to discover themselves. But what is different about my students is that they often have their incarceration to contend with.

One of the chief tools I have to combat this is my individual relationships with each of them. Before we learn a single formula or equation, I try to convey that I see them as people, not kids in the criminal justice system. My hope is that once they know this, they can start to trust me, and from there, we can turn to academics. Prepandemic, I would foster this dynamic in many ways: kneeling beside their desks, offering quiet one-on-one space, checking in with every student each day. But when the pandemic hit, all that changed. My toolbox disappeared.

While teachers I knew in traditional schools were Zooming, I wasn't allowed to take advantage of the technology so many teachers across the world had access to. I assembled lessons in paper packets, crossing my fingers that some of the curriculum would land. When we were finally allowed to meet remotely, it was via speakerphone, as we were told video was a safety concern to protect their privacy.

Worst of all, my ability to connect with my students individually evaporated. I couldn't establish trust with new students, and I couldn't maintain the trust I'd built with the kids I already knew. Instead of one-on-one minimeetings crouched at their desks or the group dynamic we'd worked so hard to build, my students became silent air on a speakerphone, everyone too nervous to speak because when they did, they had to speak to the whole group.

In the fall of 2020, when I was given the choice to return to the classroom or stay remote, I jumped at the chance to go back. Of course, a lot was different. Desk crouching, for example, wasn't possible. I was used to keeping track of pencils (students weren't allowed to leave the facility with them), but now we had to keep track of pencils in a whole different way (we ended using toothbrush holders with names on them; it worked great). Incarceration is isolating to begin with, but by the time I got back to the classroom, some of my students hadn't seen their families in months. Their loneliness took up a huge amount of space in our room, manifesting in an extreme quiet that settled over our lessons.

I still don't know how long it will be until we get back to where we were or if we ever will. But it does feel, in our bedroom-sized classroom, there is more grace than before. Even though we're often invisible to the outside world, we are reminded now how lucky we are to see each other.

Danielle Kardon teaches at a program for incarcerated youth in the Northeast. She loves her job.

Six-Word Memoirs *from students in the program*

What is the world like now?

Help me. Save me. Free me.

Unfamiliar masked faces. Unmasked familiar faces.

The pandemic has ruined our lives.

 Six-Word Memoirs *from teachers*

Hate's a virus. Stop Asian hate.

Pivot. Asynchronous. Distance Learning. 2020 words.

The One where we stayed home.

Thank God the internet works today.

Mute your mic. Share your screen.

Alexa, Play wash your hands, Please.

- Zoey Valles, 5

Ok, Google,
please end the pandemic.

- Nate Mitton, 10

Hey Siri,
give me social interaction.

- Eli Mitton, 12

Can we *not* talk about
ROBLOX?

- Samantha Moss

Social isolation was obviously new for everyone. As an introvert, I didn't think I would be heavily affected by it, but I was wrong. Totally wrong. The idea of not having the option to go outside bothered me, not being able to hang out with my friends and being stuck inside twenty-four hours a day started to affect my moods and behaviors. But even apart from that, I did miss school.

Sleeping in, not being sent on errands, and binge-watching Netflix is fun and all … until it's the only thing you can do for an entire year! At some point you get tired of these things and start learning and thinking more about yourself, who you really are, and what's really important to you.

Being stuck at home for all that time forced me to start to pay attention to what was happening in our world, specifically the Black Lives Matter movement and the great injustice that the black community has faced for a very long time. It's sad to say that it took me being stuck in my own home to make me more attentive to all the world changing events that have been taking place.

Being stuck at home with my family at the beginning of the pandemic gave me both an understanding of the movement and a chance to learn about my parents' and siblings' perspectives on the BLM protests. My parents are very traditional, and so they weren't very passionate about the movement. In their eyes, everyone was at fault. The Black community. The cops. The government. Everybody was doing something wrong.

Part of me agreed with my parents. Still, I had to keep in mind that my parents and I belong to different generations. We find different things "important." I started to learn more about the history of the black community and more about what we have been through throughout the years. My younger brother also started to learn about the issues, and we were able to discuss them.

One of the reasons I'm looking forward to getting back to school is because I can continue to discuss these things. As a Black woman, I'm learning that being silent isn't going to help the cause. The pandemic has been rough on everyone, and it seems to me it's been even rougher on communities of color, but if there's a silver lining to the pandemic, it's that now I can see that that lining is actually Black.

Shanette Addison attends Bard High School Early College in New York City.

On the Board and Off, Together

By *Meg Mullins*

Halfway through the 2020 school year I challenged my students to document what the pandemic experience had been like through their eyes in six words for future generations to read. They wrote about missed events, changing academic protocols, friendships they missed, adjustments to their daily routines, and new skills they learned. They wrote honestly about the impact these changes had on their mental health and shared their profound sense of loss. As a final step to our project, we exchanged our memoirs, peer-editing style, and students were able to help distill each other's experiences. When we settled on our final drafts, I took each of their six words and wrote them out on a colorful tag, arranging them together in an overlapping bulletin for all of us to see. Even if we couldn't be close to each other, our experiences could be—and were—both on the board and off.

Meg Mullins is an 11th grade ELA teacher at Roy C Ketcham, Wappingers Central School District in Hopewell Junction, NY

Life during Coronatime, in SIX WORDS.

Three pandemic jobs:
waitress, lifeguard, educator.

- Erin Scussel, teacher

I am working. I'm researching *sleep.*

- Lola Seiter, 11

Learned a lot about
online shopping.

- Michael Lozada

Too overworked to be
so ineffective.

- Jennifer Garwood, teacher

I came.
    I taught.
        I retired.

- Maureen Prendergast, teacher

Done with teaching into the void.

- Emilie King, teacher

Dream job: *teaching.*
Pandemic nightmare: *teaching.*

- Cristina Heredia, teacher

Weak internet connections.
Strong classroom connections.

- Emily Miller, teacher

- Afton Shumate, Kansas City Art Institute

Pros: at home.
Cons: at home.

- Alex Bruno

Hallway hike, bathtub swim, Pandora concert.

- Susan Evind

My room: sometimes bedroom, sometimes classroom.

- Mary Rogelie Magbanua, 20

Not enough sweatpants for this gig.

- Laura Fraser

Dear Diary,

nothing new for now.

- Mellyzza Carlyne Catingub

Days repeat themselves without
an end.

- Brooklyn Durant, 10

I am surrounded, yet I'm alone.

- Finn Yang, 10

Maybe hard,
but we survived this!

- Dylan Berger, 10

The world is a fragile place.

- Ben Cohen-Vigder, 10

Tired.

This making history is

exhausting.

- Teri Porter

Another day,
	another viewing of *Frozen*.

> *- Trey Hensley*

Masks on. Zoom off. Let's play!

> *- Evie Brown, 6*

Graduated fourth grade from
my bedroom.

> *- Leo Feldman, 9*

"Mama!"

"What?"

"Mama!"

"What?"

"Never mind."

> *- Cathy Alter, mother of Leo*

Hugging:
  grandchildren,
    children,
      friends.
        In order.

- Sherry Ainscough

Come in my head for company.

- Bee Brown, 13

Darkness descends and
devours my teenager.

- Amy Brown, Bee's mom

A learning curve for us all.

- Eugene Sanchez

Hardest Things Today, Won't Be Tomorrow

By Candra McKenzie

To teach in New York City is a badge of honor, but when you have to coteach physics through a pandemic, virtually, it's a whole other challenge.

Before school began, I had reflected on my own experience learning physics as a teenager and how complex a subject it was. I could only imagine that with schools partially opened and no labs for students to conduct experiments in how difficult it was going to be teach, but my coteacher and I pushed on. We recorded videos and used interactive software, but as the year wore on, it became harder for students to absorb the material and engage in class.

For one thing, the virus was ravaging our Black and Brown communities, not only taking lives but revealing the poverty of many students. Students who once showed their faces started to be silent and many decided to hide behind a celebrity photo. In addition to having less and less student interaction, it became increasingly clear that physics was a subject that really needed a kinesthetic approach.

We couldn't make psychics more physically accessible, but we could show our students people who looked like them demonstrating what physics was all about. After scouring the web for organizations that supported Black and Brown scientists, scanning university faculty pages, and sending numerous emails, I received more responses than I could imagine.

Our online science class became a revolving door of physicists. We had an astrophysicist show images of the sun from space while speaking Spanish and Portuguese. A doctoral student discussed how Neil deGrasse Tyson isn't the *only* ambassador for science. Another guest speaker spoke about his Senegalese background and introduced his college-aged daughter who is studying physics. One guest, Dr. Miguel Castro-Colin, explained how physicists look at chocolate bars in order to create better taste. He then offered advice, "The hardest thing today, won't be the hardest thing tomorrow." Suddenly teaching online became accessible and physics became attainable.

The students could see themselves in our speakers and became willing to talk to us about what they didn't understand. It was the spark they needed to see that science was not a barrier but a way of opening doors. And my coteacher and I saw that science wasn't just about sharing information but about displaying relevance to our lives.

The pandemic challenged all of us to think outside our classroom walls. My students were able to see the field of science as a portal to the world, and I and my fellow teachers were able to recognize that as we return to in-person school, we should continue to look to allies to enhance education. If the pandemic taught us anything it's that "the hardest things today, won't be tomorrow".

Candra McKenzie is a New York City public school teacher and, as Ms. Mac, hosts the educational podcast "HallPassBreak."

Six-Word Memoirs *by a few of Ms. McKenzie's students*

It was hard, but not impossible. - *Jared Aguilar Turcios*

Blinded by all the blue lights. - *Sire Simon*

I thought about giving up. Nevermind. - *Wilbert Cummings*

Everyday, physics became harder and harder. - *Alpha Diallo*

- *Talon Newton, Kansas City Art Institute*

- Camille Conner, Kansas City Art Institute

our
fates intertwine
with
mother earth

Pandemic couldn't stop my birthday celebration!

- Justine Ray Alcuizar, 14

COVID-19 taught us **resilience** amidst adversities.

- Ray Alcuizar, Justine's dad

Post pandemic – more friends, family, favorites.

- Caleb Potts, 8

Post pandemic - reconnecting, restoring, and revitalizing.

- John Pott, Caleb's dad

I'm busy at camp
forgetting it.

- Maggie Daiber, 17

One year, two kids,
five schools

- Dave Daiber, Maggie's dad

Pandemic ends, my frontal
lobe returns.

- Ruth Milligan, Maggie's mom

Exercise in futility: P.E. on Zoom.

- *Elsie Thompson, 14*

Yeah, I'm gonna need another beer.

- *Bryce Fish, P.E. teacher*

Sold home, emptied nest,
bought sailboat.

- Andrew Adams

Moving forward. Standing
still. Peloton spins.

- Rabbi Lisa Gelber

Putting on clothes was my cardio.

- Jenny Mollen

Year filled with magnificence
and
desolation.

- Zoie Glosson, 12

My pandemic passion:
learned to DJ.

- Alexander Lehmann-Haupt, 8

Kid's beats:
soundtrack to our quarantine.

- Rachel Lehmann-Haupt, Alexander's mom

I played Legos all day long.

- George Macy, 5

Sex therapist's books.
Kindergarten Zoom
backround.

- Jess Levith, George's mom

Breakfast
     SNACK
          Lunch
               SNACK
                    Dinner
                         SNACK

- Isa Bijl Thompson, 11

**Finally finished YouTube.
Ending is disappointing.**

- Clara Bijl, Isa's mom

BIG books are the best ones.

- Nat Androphy, 6

Two parents. Two kids. One bathroom.

- Dina Mann, Nat's mom

JUST DREAMING THIS ENDLESS WINTER AWAY

- Althes Flores, Kansas City Art Institute

FUTURE PATHS REVEALED THEMSELVES, IN TIME.

- *David Terrill, Kansas City Art Institute, Associate Professor*

Despondent Daughters +
Desperate Dad = DIY Camp

By Randall Lane

It started, as with many half-baked ideas, with an ad I secretly took out on Craigslist: *Math Tutor Needed*. Those who clicked quickly discovered the fine print: you needed to live in a bubble house in the Catskills with a dozen girls and a divorced dad for the entire month of August. Craigslist being Craigslist, a few dozen people applied. There wasn't actually a bubble or a mountain house or a dozen girls. Yet. But the biggest hurdle now market-validated, I was emboldened.

I was also desperate. While quarantine sucked for everyone, for me, nothing stung more than watching my thirteen- and sixteen-year-old daughters physically isolated from their peers at the exact moment when human beings are designed to sprout social wings. COVID summer was another level of hell, especially as any novelty had passed, along with the diversion that passed for online schoolwork. My youngest had been excited for her first sleepaway camp; my oldest got into a leadership program at Brown. Both canceled, the girls were staring at a summer of…nothing.

Enter DIY Camp. If every kid was now a shut-in, why not shut a handful of them together in a place that could just happen to boast hiking and swimming and math? And most importantly, a chance to feel normal.

With trust paramount, I kept the group to just my daughters and their friends. The other parents were understandably skeptical. But as quarantine provided endless thinking time, I had endless answers, from precamp quarantines and testing, to co-op cost splits and no-phone dictates(!). The sharp Craigslist math tutor (she proved an excellent STEM role model) came with a Marxist boyfriend, who would serve as activities director/nurse (he got a Red Cross certification online). I found a giant lakehouse on Airbnb, a new volleyball net on Amazon, and a trampoline on eBay.

Most miraculously of all, everything pretty much worked. The girls, overwhelmed to be together IRL, eschewed their devices and spent the month collaborating and competing and laughing and crying. We watched meteor showers and made bonfires and held talent nights. In other words, we were human again. Or they were at least. I was just exhausted.

I was also gratified. The first surprising dividend wasn't that they had a great August; it's that they spent the months before obsessing about every detail, which mitigated the pandemic boredom in May, June, and July, too.

The second, and perhaps the sweetest surprise of this endeavor, was that even after vaccinations provided a return to near-normalcy in time for summer 2021, the entire younger cohort, now with a world of choices, requested something rarely heard during this tough time in our lives: they wanted to relive it again.

Randall Lane is the Chief Content Officer of Forbes Media and editor of Forbes *Magazine.*

It was a time of opportunities.

- Sydney Anderson, 12

I'm possible

was found in *impossible*.

- Sabrina Anderson, 12

Reinventing instruction,
  assessment,
   purpose,
   and meaning.

- Michelle Anderson,
teacher and mom to Sydney and Sabrina

"After the pandemic."
An odd concept.

- Maggie Rice, 13

```
Teacher quit
      to help
    her mom.
```

- Ian Rice, 11

Addled dad quickly became just "d'addled."

- Neil Rice, Maggie and Ian's dad

You can't make me go outside.

- Jacqueline Rice, Maggie and Ian's aunt

We're already
homeschooled.
We still heroes?

- *John Paul White*

Seven years' homeschooling
FINALLY pays off.

- *Karen D. Hirsch*

Never wanted to be home schooled.

- *Paulina Simon*

At least our dog learned geography.

- *Scott and Caroline Simon, Paulina's parents*

No longer the weird
homeschooling family.

- Keith Knight

Inside my house and my head.

- *Cassie Kuenn, 17*

The dog now thinks
I'm agoraphobic.

- *Ivy Sandz, teacher*

Well, my cats loved the company.

- *Grace Villa Loyer*

Really been wishing on time travel.

- *Hanna Docampo Pham, 13*

Time with my two teenagers — PRICELESS.

- Rick Smolan

To boomers:
we had it *worse*.

- Kai Lua De Souza, 17

- Lazarre Elias, 8

- Simone Elias, 11

By Julie Taylor

I have been a literacy specialist for twenty-five years. When I learned about the Six-Word Memoir project and introduced the form to my students, I witnessed how this "American Haiku" unlocked students' creativity. During the pandemic, I taught students about diction, syntax, and connotation and then had each one write a Six-Word Memoir about how it felt to be a middle school student during this very hard time in their lives.

I've never been one to settle for small projects and soon realized we were making history, so why not include the whole school and record their memoirs in a book? The eighth graders were already reading *The Diary of Anne Frank,* so creating a book full of memories for future generations to read seemed too fitting. So that's what we did. Five, ten, twenty, fifty years from now, we will have a book called *Pandemic 2020: Caught in the Middle* in our Ashe libraries to help us remember. Here are their stories, shared in our book, and now in yours, too.

Julie Taylor is the Director of K-12 Curriculum and Federal Programs, Ashe County Schools, North Carolina

from Ms. Taylor's students

Life is spicy, COVID is tasteless. - *Brody B.*

How can emptiness feel so heavy? - *Lincoln H.*

No school, no sports, only distance. - *Landen W.*

No visitors allowed; depression explodes daily. - *Hayden B.*

Turning friends to strangers…all alone. - *Chelsea P.*

My cat is tired of me. - *Titus P.*

Not happy. Not sad. Just empty. - *Tristan N.*

Mask: you take my breath away. - *Isabella F.*

The year the toilet paper disappeared. - *Hannah O.*

Remember when only doctors wore masks? - *Robert M.*

Used to have A's—not anymore. - *Noah W.*

Online school: a portal to procrastination. - *Atlantis J.*

Slowmo day but in real time. - *Tristan F.*

Social distancing is this introvert's dream! - *Phoebe W.*

I turn in work at 2 a.m. - *Lanie B.*

Never thought loneliness hurt so much. - *Luke O.*

Don't know whether to hug grandma. - *Evie P.*

Is boredom a symptom of Covid? - *Isaac F.*

Dissatisfaction has been the greatest teacher. - *Ben C.*

Youthful giggles turned into masked tears. - *Zoey L.*

We're aware you're stressed. More homework? - *Lucas O.*

Now or later? Later it is! - *Kaitlyn M.*

I didn't get Covid…or guys! - *Amelia L.*

Which mask should I wear today? - *Brooklyn L.*

I'm fine, I'm fine, I'm fine. - *Carson P.*

Maybe there's hope I can't see. - *Emily E.*

Silent school hallways; saddest sound ever. - *Julie Taylor*

Changing DAY pajamas to
NIGHT pajamas.

- Easter Dodds

Boy, these sweatpants really got **snug**.

- Rob Simons, former teacher

I miss not needing to quarantine.

- Kestrel Thomas, 6

Make your bed
and
get dressed.

- Elizabeth Gilbert

At last, seeing friends in 3-D.

- *Charlotte Cranmer*

That's what youʀ face Looks Like?

- *Shelby Hardin*

Reconnecting
and
connecting with six words.

- *Alexie Puran*

Numbers rose, but SUN did, too.

- *Paloma Lenz*

Teachers on Teaching
Six-Word Memoirs

"The limitation of six words forces students to break big ideas down to smaller bites, think deeper about their stories, and unlock personal expression. I've seen kids work through writer's block. In just thirty minutes they feel like they have accomplished something."

—Terry Ashkinos, middle school humanities teacher, Children's Day School, San Francisco

"As a teaching literacy specialist of 25 years who has moved into district curriculum planning, I have seen the many powerful ways that this 'American Haiku' format can unlock students' creativity. Incorporating these lessons has helped our teachers understand how the students feel, and everyone has loved the chance for our students to see themselves as published authors."

—Julie Taylor, Director of K-12 Curriculum and Federal Programs, Ashe County Schools, North Carolina

"The day I used Six-Word Memoirs was the day my students came alive. Being free to write in this wonderful short format helped them to discover the essence of themselves and the heart of their writing."

— Candra McKenzie, English and ESL NYC public school teacher and host of the podcast, HallPassBreak

"My students especially love the Six-Word Memoir form because they love structure. Somehow the rules create and allow a structured freedom of sorts."

—*Meghan Adler, learning and literacy specialist*

"The Six-Word Memoir is the perfect instrument for students to exercise their self-awareness in meaningful ways. Having this type of personal success on the first assignment of the school year sets the tone for a positive and productive year."

—*Elizabeth Kennedy, Seventh Grade Academic Enrichment Instructor, Riverwatch Middle School in Suwanee, Georgia.*

Read hundreds of stories about how teachers bring Six-Word Memoirs into their classrooms at

sixinschools.com

LARRY SMITH is the founder of the Six-Word Memoir Project, a bestselling series of books, live event programs, and a global phenomenon found in classrooms, conferences, and corporate settings alike. He's a frequent speaker on the power of personal storytelling and has engaged teams at Twitter, Levi's, JPMorgan Chase, Snapchat, Dell, Shutterfly, and ESPN, as well as foundations, philanthropies, and schools around the world. Larry produced and directed *A Map of Myself*, the true story of young Palestinian-Syrian-American woman's journey from Syria to America that started with her Six-Word Memoir, "Escaped war; war never escaped me." Called on "a quest to spark the creativity in everyone" by *Oprah Magazine*, Larry proudly wears his Six-Word Memoir on his sleeve (and his t-shirt): "Big hair, big heart, big hurry."